2012 – 2016
Border Patrol Strategic Plan

The Mission: Protect America

U.S. Customs and Border Protection

U.S. BORDER PATROL

U.S. Customs and
Border Protection

2012-2016 Border Patrol Strategic Plan

Table of Contents

Goals, Objectives, Strategies, Programs, and Initiatives

MESSAGE FROM THE ACTING COMMISSIONER

The 2012-2016 Border Patrol Strategic Plan marks an important point in the growth and development of the U.S. Border Patrol. The Strategic Plan establishes an approach for the Border Patrol that is tailored to meet the challenges of securing a 21st century border against a variety of different threats and adversaries. The 2012-2016 Strategic Plan builds on the foundation of the 2004 National Border Patrol Strategy, which guided the acquisition and deployment of significant additional resources – personnel, technology, and infrastructure – to support execution of the Border Patrol's mission.

The resource base built and the operations conducted over the past two decades have enabled the Border Patrol to focus on developing and implementing a Strategic Plan based on risk: identifying high risk areas and flows and targeting our response to meet those threats. This risk-based approach is reflected in the core pillars of the Strategic Plan – Information, Integration and Rapid Response. These pillars are central to the 21st century Border Patrol we continue to build. Information and intelligence will empower Border Patrol leadership and agents to get ahead of the threat and to be predictive and proactive. Integration of effort with the range of partners with whom we work will ensure we bring all available capabilities and tools to bear in addressing threats. Through Rapid Response, we will deploy resources timely and effectively to meet and mitigate the threats we confront.

The 2012 Strategic Plan continues a history of innovation and evolution of the Border Patrol. Beginning with Operation Hold the Line in El Paso in 1993 and Operation Gatekeeper in San Diego in 1994, the Border Patrol began strategically deploying resources to meet the highest priority threats. These operations and those based on them that followed were significantly successful. As a result of the Border Patrol and other agencies' efforts, the Southwest Border is more secure today than it has ever been. The Strategic Plan draws on these earlier applications of a risk-based approach, and as part of the overall effort of U.S. Customs and Border Protection (CBP) and other agencies, will help ensure that we continue making progress in securing our borders.

The evolution of the Border Patrol as a risk-based, intelligence-driven law enforcement organization is part of a much larger change in the U.S. Government's approach to border and homeland security. The September 11, 2001 terrorist attacks initiated a fundamental rethinking about cross-border movements and security, including border security. The creation of the Department of Homeland Security (DHS) and CBP were critical structural changes. CBP was formed through the merger of four separate organizations from three separate cabinet departments into one new agency: the U.S. Border Patrol and the port inspections component of the Immigration and Naturalization Service from the Department of Justice, dealing with people seeking to enter the country legally and illegally; the U.S. Customs Service from the U.S. Department of the Treasury, dealing with cargo and goods; and the Agriculture Inspection Service from the Department of Agriculture, dealing with agricultural pests and potential infestation of our crop lands.

The scope of the border protection mission was sharpened and honed: keeping dangerous people and dangerous things away from the American homeland, especially terrorists and terrorist weapons. Our job at CBP, in large measure, is to secure the flows of goods and people moving toward and intending to enter the United States. At the core of our approach to securing flows is assessing and managing risk. In the Strategic Plan, the Border Patrol is applying the principles of risk management to its mission set. CBP has made tremendous progress since its formation in addressing and working through the implications of unified border management and the border security mission, but we remain a work in progress. The Strategic Plan sets a firm foundation for the continued evolution of the Border Patrol as an integral part of CBP's overall border management and homeland security enterprise.

The Strategic Plan reflects and builds on the transformation of the United States' relationships with Mexico and Canada, particularly in the areas of border management and security. The joint Declaration of Principles for the 21st-century border represents an enhanced and strengthened commitment to fundamentally restructure the way we manage our shared border. The depth and breadth of cooperation that occurs now between the United States and Mexico was unthinkable even a few years ago. Similarly, the Beyond the Border declaration between Canada and the United States has an equally significant potential in what is already our historically extraordinary relationship with Canada. These developments have created unprecedented opportunities with both Mexico and Canada, in which DHS and CBP will play a defining role, to improve our security and economic competitiveness – and CBP will play a defining role in taking advantage of those opportunities. The Border Patrol in turn is key to advancing CBP's security agendas with Mexico and Canada, working with its law enforcement counterparts in each country to identify and mitigate threats.

The U.S. Border Patrol is a premier law enforcement organization, recognized around the world for expertise, capabilities, and professionalism. CBP's officers and agents are the frontline, the guardians of the Nation's borders. We honor and are proud of them, and we thank them for everything that they do to protect America and the American people.

David V. Aguilar
Acting Commissioner

U.S. Customs and
Border Protection

U.S. Customs and Border Protection

CBP Mission Statement

We are the guardians of our Nation's borders.
We are America's frontline.

We safeguard the American homeland at and beyond our borders.

We protect the American public against terrorists and the instruments of terror.

We steadfastly enforce the laws of the United States while fostering our Nation's economic security through lawful international trade and travel.

We serve the American public with vigilance, integrity, and professionalism.

CBP Core Values

Vigilance is how we ensure the safety of all Americans. We are continuously watchful and alert to deter, detect and prevent threats to our Nation. We demonstrate courage and valor in the protection of our Nation.

Service to Country is embodied in the work we do. We are dedicated to defending and upholding the Constitution of the United States. The American people have entrusted us to protect the homeland and defend liberty.

Integrity is our cornerstone. We are guided by the highest ethical and moral principles. Our actions bring honor to ourselves, our agency, and our country.

MESSAGE FROM THE CHIEF

The U.S. Border Patrol is entering an exciting new era. The 2012-2016 Border Patrol Strategic Plan offers every Border Patrol agent and support staff member the opportunity to enhance their role in ensuring the security of our Nation's borders.

The September 11, 2001 terrorist attacks against our Nation defined U.S. Customs and Border Protection's national security mission: nothing less than preventing terrorists and terrorist weapons from entering the United States.

The world has changed during the last decade, and so have the threats that we face every day. We have seen these changes from Imperial Beach, California, to Brownsville, Texas; from Blaine, Washington, to Van Buren, Maine; and from Lake Charles, Louisiana, to Ramey, Puerto Rico. After assimilation into the new Department of Homeland Security and CBP, and having experienced unprecedented organizational growth, the Border Patrol is stronger than it has ever been.

After years of deploying resources, like infrastructure, and technology, we are about to put these enhanced capabilities to the most effective use with the implementation of the 2012-2016 Border Patrol Strategic Plan.

The principal theme of the Strategic Plan is to use **Information, Integration, and Rapid Response** to meet all threats. We will build upon an approach that puts the Border Patrol's greatest capabilities in place to combat the greatest risks. We will gather and analyze **Information,** ensure **Integration** through operational planning and execution with our international, Federal, state, local, and tribal law enforcement partners, and based on risk, deploy the appropriate **Rapid Response** to the threat.

This means that as threats evolve and risks fluctuate, the Border Patrol will adapt and respond quickly.

Of course, to reach our full potential, we must continue to invest in our most valuable asset – the men and women of the Border Patrol. Along with protecting our citizens, there is no greater responsibility.

I want to thank each of you for your outstanding commitment to excellence and dedication to duty. As I have traveled to the field, I have had the opportunity to talk with many of you. I know and certainly appreciate the personal sacrifices that you and your families have made to protect America, and for that I remain eternally grateful. While the future brings many challenges, I am confident that all of you will meet these challenges. Working together, we will overcome them. It is indeed an honor and a privilege to be working with you as we protect this great Nation.

Honor First!

Michael J. Fisher

Michael J. Fisher
Chief
U.S. Border Patrol

"We provide the ability to identify and minimize risk, and to respond quickly should a risk materialize."
— *Secretary Janet Napolitano.* <u>Washington Post</u>, April 22, 2010.

EXECUTIVE SUMMARY

2004: A Resource-Based Strategy

The Border Patrol's 2004 Strategy focused on getting the Border Patrol organized and resourced to meet its new, post-9/11 mission and succeed in its new parent organization. The 2004 Strategy achieved impressive results. For instance, it organized the Border Patrol into a more centralized and Headquarters-driven organization. Furthermore, it facilitated the unprecedented deployment of personnel, technology, and infrastructure to secure the Nation's borders.

2012: A Risk-Based Strategic Plan

The 2012-2016 Strategic Plan supports national-level strategies, such as the President's Strategy to Combat Transnational Organized Crime and the National Drug Control Strategy; departmental strategies, in particular the Quadrennial Homeland Security Review; and CBP-wide planning and integration efforts. The Strategic Plan uses a risk-based approach to securing the border; focusing enhanced capabilities against the highest threats and rapidly responding along the border. It involves a set of objectives, strategies, and programs that use **Information, Integration and Rapid Response** to develop and deploy new and better tactics, techniques, and procedures to achieve the Border Patrol's strategic objectives. It means being more effective and efficient by using tools and methods like change-detection techniques to mitigate risks. It also means continued integration within CBP and working with Federal, state, local, tribal, and international partners.

The Strategic Plan has two interrelated and interdependent goals. In the first goal, the Border Patrol will work with its Federal, state, local, tribal, and international partners to secure the border using **Information, Integration and Rapid Response** in a risk-based manner. **Information** provides situational awareness and intelligence developed by blending things such as reconnaissance, sign-cutting and tracking, and technology to understand the threats faced along the Nation's borders. **Integration** denotes CBP corporate planning and execution of border-security operations while leveraging partnerships with other Federal, state, local, tribal, and international organizations. **Rapid Response** means the Border Patrol and its partners can respond quickly and appropriately to changing threats.

The second goal of the Strategic Plan represents an investment in people and organizational capabilities. This means improving the skills and abilities of personnel, optimizing organizational structures and processes, and becoming a more mature and sophisticated law enforcement organization.

Integration across all components of CBP within the goals of the Strategic Plan is essential. At both the tactical and strategic levels, the U.S. Border Patrol continually participates in unified efforts, such as corridor campaigns and intelligence collaboration that facilitate contiguous border-security operations.

Goal 1: Secure America's Borders

The U.S. Border Patrol plays a critical role in securing our Nation's borders between Ports of Entry (POEs) against all threats. We approach this mission from a risk-based orientation, allowing the Border Patrol to apply **Information, Integration and Rapid Response** in the most targeted, effective, and efficient manner. The measurable objectives of this goal are to:

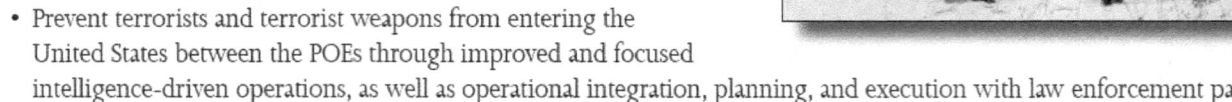

- Prevent terrorists and terrorist weapons from entering the United States between the POEs through improved and focused intelligence-driven operations, as well as operational integration, planning, and execution with law enforcement partners;
- Manage risk through the introduction and expansion of sophisticated tactics, techniques, and procedures. These include methods of detecting illegal entries such as using "change detection" techniques, increased mobile-response capabilities, and expanded use of specially trained personnel with "force multiplying" skills and abilities;
- Disrupt and degrade Transnational Criminal Organizations by targeting enforcement efforts against the highest priority threats and expanding programs that reduce smuggling and crimes associated with smuggling;
- Expand CBP's situational awareness at and between the POEs and employ a comprehensive and integrated "whole-of-government" approach; and
- Increase community engagement by participating in community programs and engaging the public to assist the U.S. Border Patrol.

Goal 2: Strengthen the Border Patrol

To succeed in its border-security mission, the Border Patrol must continue to evolve and improve as an organization using **Information, Integration and Rapid Response.** The Border Patrol will grow and mature its institutional capabilities by:

- Strengthening its investment in its people and capabilities through improved education, training, and support of Border Patrol personnel;
- Reinforcing employee-support initiatives and programs that continue the tradition of the U.S. Border Patrol;
- Addressing threats to organizational integrity and remaining vigilant in training and promoting initiatives to combat corruption;
- Improving organizational processes, systems, and doctrine by standardizing reporting and planning processes;
- Introducing improved tools to collect and analyze data to develop measures for the improvement of organizational outcomes; and
- Enhancing overall efficiency by improving planning, resource allocation, and acquisition processes.

Goal 1: Secure America's Borders

Protecting the Nation's borders – land, air, and sea – from the illegal entry of people, weapons, drugs, and contraband is vital to homeland security, as well as economic prosperity. The U.S. Border Patrol plays a pivotal role in securing the border between the Ports of Entry. This Strategic Plan will leverage **Information, Integration and Rapid Response** to secure the Nation's borders against all types of illegal entries in a manner that is risk-based and prioritizes capabilities against the highest threats.

Objective 1.1

Prevent Terrorists and Terrorist Weapons from Entering the United States

The attacks on September 11, 2001 gave rise to the Department of Homeland Security (DHS) and the many agencies, including CBP, which came together under this new Department. The U.S. Border Patrol plays a significant part

in this collaborative and critical effort. The Border Patrol conducts operations based on current intelligence and threats to prevent the entry of terrorists and terrorist weapons across U.S. borders.

Intelligence-Driven Operations

Identifying and developing a comprehensive understanding of terrorist and transnational criminal threats to the Nation's borders is paramount in accomplishing the Border Patrol's mission. We must operate by strategically using intelligence to ensure that Border Patrol operations are focused and targeted against potential terrorist threats and against TCOs. To accomplish the Border Patrol's mandated mission, we must continue to integrate intelligence and enforcement capabilities into the planning and execution of CBP operations.

Intelligence Synthesis

The current risk environment in which the Border Patrol and other law enforcement agencies operate is characterized by a variety of constantly evolving terrorist and transnational criminal threats that are both complex and varying.

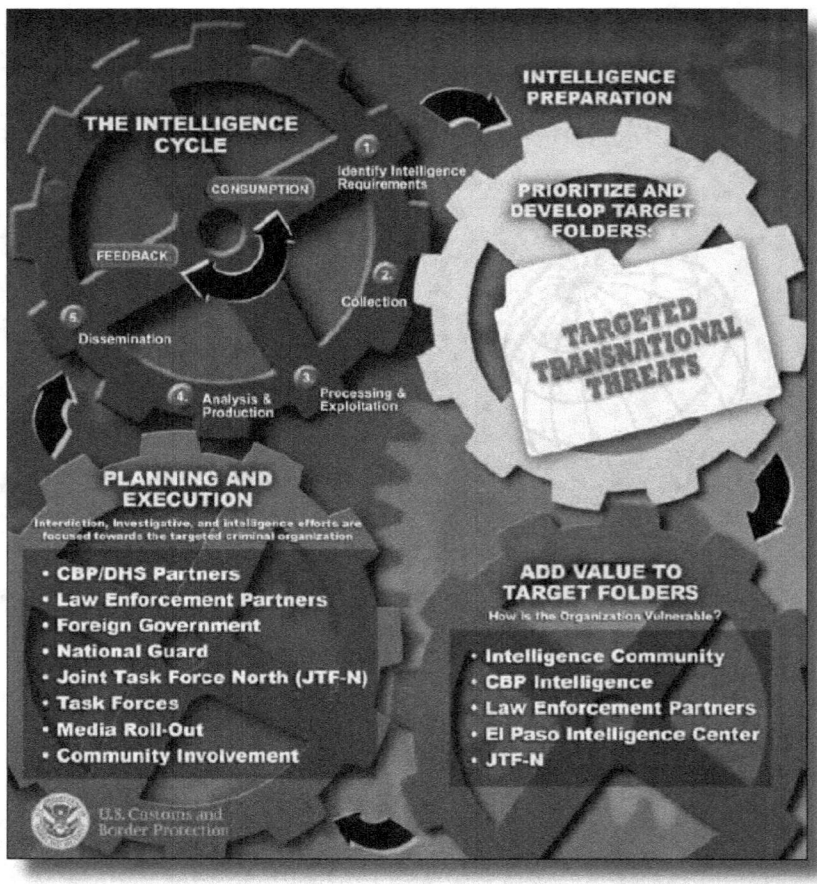

The capacity to develop timely, well-formulated, and actionable intelligence is vital to the prevention and disruption of threats. The Border Patrol will meet this challenge by supporting an integrated intelligence platform that promotes information sharing throughout the domestic and foreign law enforcement community. This endeavor is accomplished through the integration and support of Border Patrol intelligence frameworks and other intelligence entities such as the CBP Office of Intelligence and Investigative Liaison, the El Paso Intelligence Center's Border Intelligence Fusion Section, Border Intelligence Centers, and the interagency Human Smuggling and Trafficking Center, as well as state and major urban area Fusion Centers.

Foreign Law Enforcement Agency Partnerships

Coordination with our foreign law enforcement partners is important to the Nation's security. By assisting international partners with gathering and analyzing information and intelligence, and increasing the efficiency of their operations, terrorist and transnational criminal threats – and their networks – can be identified and interdicted before they reach the borders of the United States. For these reasons, the Border Patrol works in coordination with the CBP Office of International Affairs to deploy uniquely qualified

Border Patrol subject-matter experts abroad to conduct assessments of other nations' border security, border-security forces, and training needs. Border Patrol agents are often requested to provide specialized training that is tailored to the specific needs of partner nations. Basic training missions include Border Patrol presentations of tactical skills and "table-top exercises" sponsored by various U.S. Government entities, including the Department of State and the Department of Defense (DOD). The Border Patrol also provides training support to other Federal agencies operating in partner nations.

International Liaison

As the Nation's border-security efforts have expanded beyond its physical border region, cooperation through assigned liaisons with our Canadian and Mexican partners has become an integral part of daily operations. Border Patrol agents liaise with foreign federal, state, local, and tribal agencies to enhance threat awareness, coordinate interdiction efforts, perform joint patrols and preventative operations, respond to border violence, and pursue prosecution of actors within transnational criminal organizations that seek to exploit jurisdictional borders.

The International Liaison Unit (ILU) is a national program that fosters local partnerships, trust, and mutual understanding between the Border Patrol and the Government of Mexico to increase border cooperation, security, and safety. For example, in addition to daily interaction with their counterparts, the ILU initiates monthly meetings with its Mexican partners to discuss mutual concerns and facilitate exercises that test the joint-response capabilities and coordination to catastrophic events, while increasing local communication on issues such as border violence, repatriation issues, and officer safety. International Border Enforcement Teams (IBET) similarly coordinate with the government of Canada to achieve the mutual goal of border security. The ILUs and IBETs facilitate information sharing between governments and agencies involved in the cooperative effort of ensuring regional safety and security.

Objective 1.2

Manage Risk

Developing and employing the best possible information and intelligence is critical to assessing and managing risk. The Border Patrol has made significant progress in securing the Nation's borders by applying personnel, technology, and infrastructure. These enhanced resources have made our borders more secure. Threats along the border continue to evolve, and likewise, CBP's capabilities to meet these threats must continue to adapt. Accordingly, as we evolve from a resource-based approach toward a risk-based approach, we must be able to focus the Border Patrol's new capabilities against the highest threats in predicting and rapidly responding to changes in risk along the border.

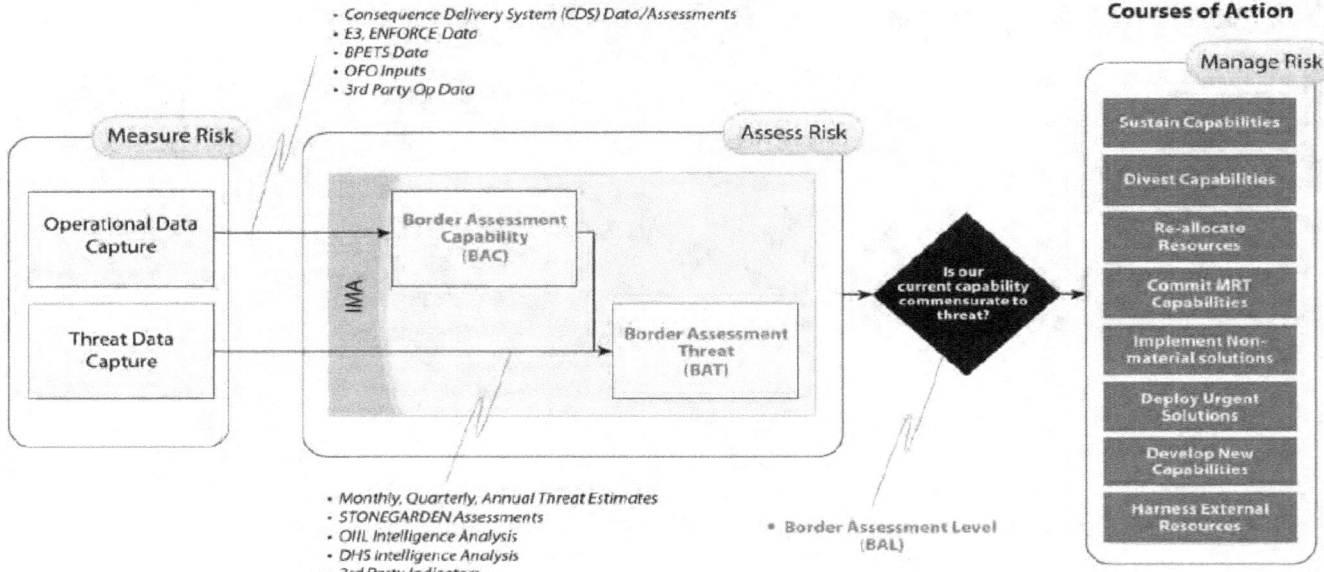

Integrated Mission Analysis

Integrated Mission Analysis (IMA) uses a systematic and comprehensive methodology to track, assess, and forecast vulnerabilities, consequences, and capabilities of CBP (and, by extension, the U.S. Border Patrol) and matches these with known or potential threats. The resulting Border Assessment Level (BAL) helps CBP answer the question: Is our capability commensurate with the threat?

The IMA process supports the Border Patrol's risk-based approach to border security by integrating operational and threat-condition assessments. Once harnessed, these operational statistics, threat indicators, and warnings will be used to estimate risk. Outputs from the IMA process will aid security stakeholders in determining operational gaps and critical threats, vulnerabilities and risks. As a result, commanders will have both the data and analysis to effectively track, assess, and forecast risk. The IMA process assists commanders in managing identified risks by allowing them to make better and timely decisions to:

- Sustain current capabilities;
- Re-allocate resources;
- Implement non-material solutions;
- Develop new capabilities;
- Divest from capabilities;
- Commit mobile-response capabilities;
- Deploy urgent solutions; and
- Harness external resources.

Mobile Response Capability

Given the dynamic nature of cross-border threats, the Border Patrol must ensure that it becomes more mobile to respond appropriately to the changing threat. This Mobile Response Capability provides the Border Patrol with the flexibility to deploy capabilities to the highest risk areas of the border. The Border Patrol also deploys scalable capabilities to areas – before they become a high risk – to maintain the highest possible levels of security in each border area. This capability builds on situational awareness, because the Border Patrol must know when, where, and to what extent to deploy its capabilities.

Mobile Response Team

The Mobile Response Team (MRT) provides a national group of organized, trained, and equipped Border Patrol agents who are capable of rapid movement to regional and national incidents and events in support of priority CBP operations. The MRT also responds to intelligence-driven targets and shifts in local and cross-border criminal activity as deemed necessary by the sector's Chief Patrol Agent. The MRT provides a flexible, enhanced, tiered-response capability to counter the emerging, changing, and evolving threats along the operational areas of the Nation's borders.

Special Operations Group

The Border Patrol Special Operations Group (SOG) is composed of two operational components: the Border Patrol Tactical Unit (BORTAC) and the Border Patrol Search, Trauma and Rescue team (BORSTAR), each with robust support and intelligence sections. SOG provides DHS, CBP, and the Border Patrol with specially trained and equipped tactical teams capable of rapid response to emergent or unusual law enforcement situations requiring special tactics and techniques, search, rescue, and medical response capabilities via land, air, and sea.

Elements of Change Detection Capability

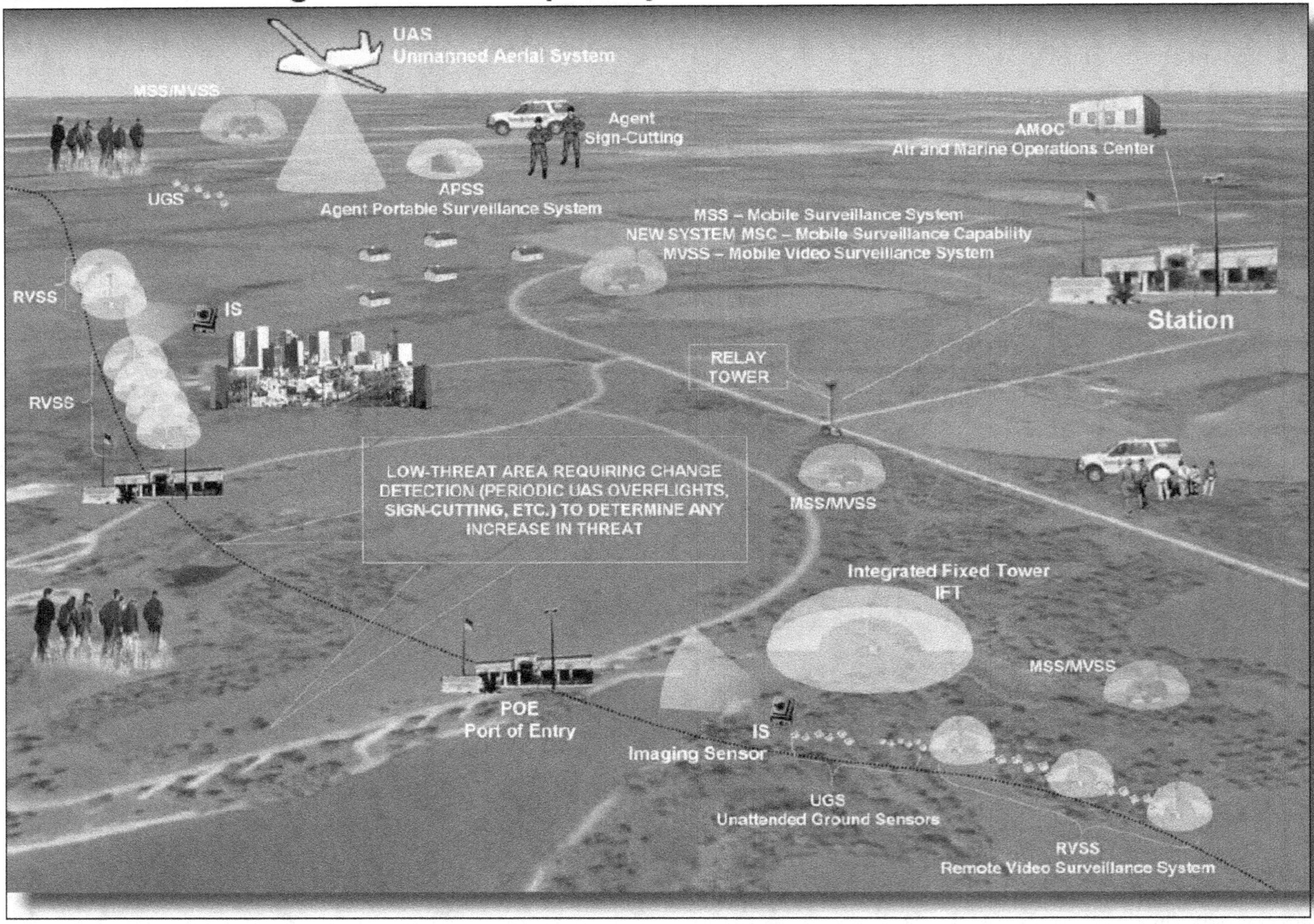

Change Detection Capability

Mobile response ensures flexibility to deploy capabilities to identified high-risk areas but it does not fully address the Border Patrol's responsibility to be vigilant in continually evaluating identified low threat areas for any changes in threat levels. Change Detection Capability is a tactical strategy using various techniques to gather information and intelligence in low-threat areas. Change Detection Capabilities increase the level of situational awareness in all areas, including those areas currently assessed as lower risk. This allows the Border Patrol to continue focusing capabilities on areas where the highest risk exists, but ensures that any threat adaptation can be identified quickly through information and intelligence, culminating in appropriate steps being taken to rapidly minimize any new risk. Periodic reconnaissance patrols, sign-cutting and tracking, Unmanned Aerial Systems (UAS) over-flights, and interaction with partners in the community are examples of programs and techniques that will be employed to determine if new threats are present in an area.

Leverage Technology

Border Patrol agents' use of technology continues to be an important capability and force multiplier for the Border Patrol and its partners. The Border Patrol leverages various forms of technology to gain situational awareness to better detect, identify, monitor, and respond to threats to the Nation's borders. Without technology, the Border Patrol cannot operate in an effective, efficient, and risk-based manner. Examples of technology now in use include:

- Biometrics
- Mobile Surveillance System (MSS)
- Mobile Video Surveillance System (MVSS)
- Remote Video Surveillance System (RVSS)
- Vehicle and Cargo Inspection System (VACIS)
- Night Vision Devices
- Thermal Hand-Held Imaging Devices
- Unattended Ground Sensors (UGS)
- Personal Radiation Detectors (PRD)
- Radiation Isotope Identification Devices (RIID)
- Z Backscatter X-Ray Vehicles
- Integrated Fixed Towers (IFT)

The Border Patrol manages its requirements for existing and emerging technology at the Headquarters level, based on input from agents in the field. The Border Patrol assesses technological needs of the mission and capability gaps, then works with its CBP partners – including the Office of Information and Technology (OIT) and Office of Technology Innovation and Acquisition (OTIA) – to manage requirements through a mission-analysis process from beginning to end. This ensures that the Border Patrol's technological needs are addressed properly through documentation, prioritization, testing, and deployment. The Border Patrol also works to identify and develop potential emerging technologies that can support current and future operational needs.

Objective 1.3

Disrupt and Degrade Transnational Criminal Organizations

Transnational criminal organizations represent a significant cross-border threat to homeland security. These organizations control most cross-border trafficking in guns and illegal drugs, as well as an increasing percentage of human smuggling. With efforts in place to understand the origin and magnitude of threats along the border, the Border Patrol can now focus on specific threats like TCOs, and work to disrupt and degrade their operations. The Border Patrol's response to this threat also will involve close collaboration within CBP and includes Federal, state, local, and tribal partners to advance the common goal of disrupting and degrading TCO activity.

Targeted Enforcement

To meet the ever-expanding and diverse threats to the Nation's borders, the Border Patrol has adopted a targeted enforcement posture to prevent and disrupt terrorist and transnational threats. Targeting threats between the POEs through intelligence and analysis translates organizational priorities into strategic, risk-based, operational plans with focused deployment of capabilities.

Due to the dynamic nature of the threats faced between the ports of entry, the Border Patrol has employed

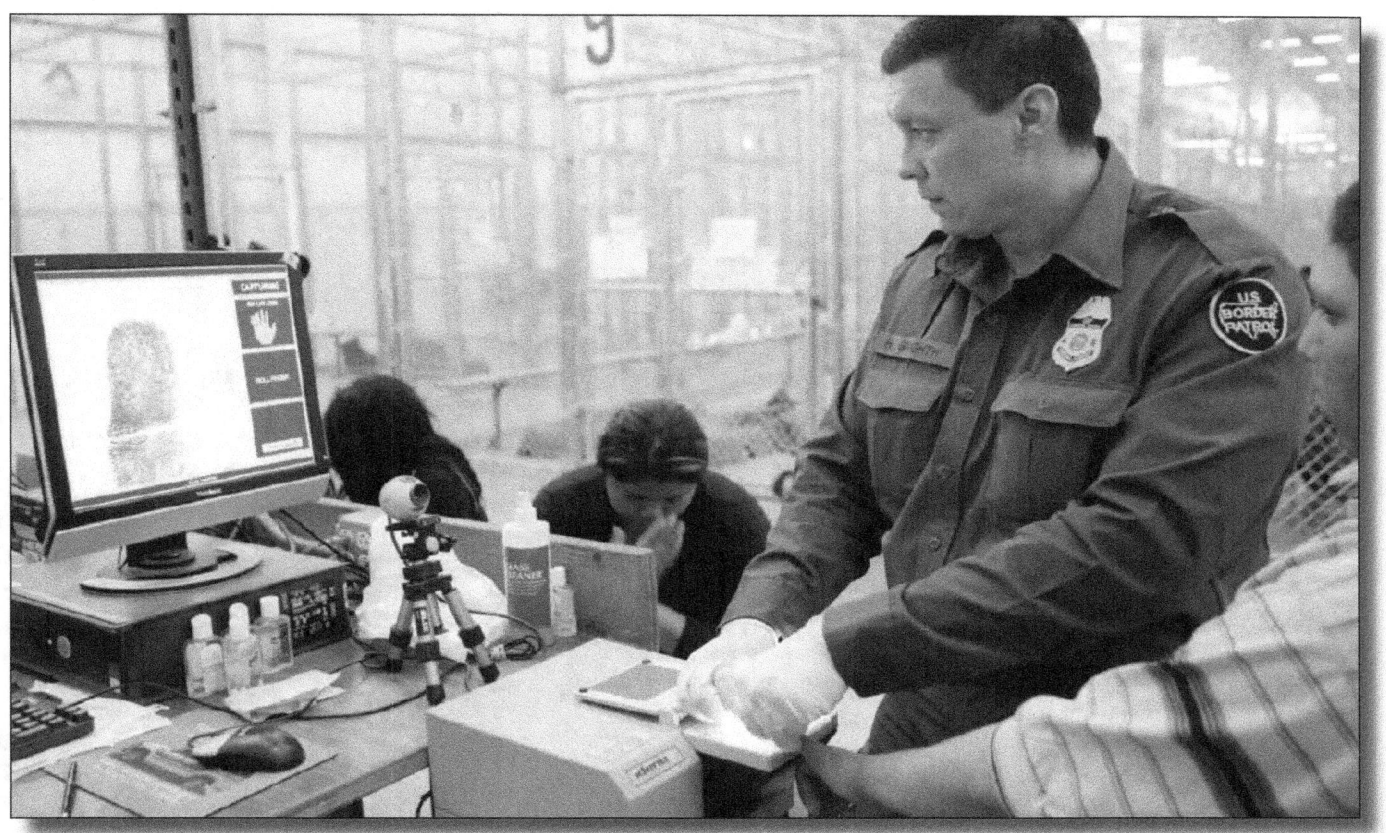

coordinated efforts to strengthen security through targeted enforcement. Through joint interagency planning, design of operations, targeting, and execution, targeted enforcement methodologies within corridors will increase the ability to disrupt and degrade TCOs along the border. Integrating with Federal and state investigative units and operating with law enforcement entities at all levels, targeted enforcement operations will have an impact on criminal operations that threaten America. Furthermore, the Border Patrol supports CBP's National Targeting Center in its efforts to use intelligence and systems to screen potential threats through the use of advanced targeting systems; providing information in an integrated approach to rapidly address the threat.

Consequence Delivery

Substantial investment in personnel, technology, and infrastructure along the Southwest Border with Mexico during the past several years has facilitated reduction of illegal cross-border activity to unprecedented levels. This reduction in traffic is now enabling the Border Patrol to manage, as opposed to simply react to, the volume of illegal traffic along our borders through the application of appropriate consequences to illegal entrants.

CBP has developed, with the support of its strategic partners, a new Consequence Delivery System (CDS) that guides management and agents through a process designed to uniquely evaluate each subject and identify the ideal consequence to break the smuggling cycle. The CDS applies effective strategies to disrupt and degrade TCOs and distribution networks. The CDS measures the consequences applied to persons illegally entering the country against defined alien classifications. CDS provides a process designed to uniquely evaluate each subject and apply the appropriate post-arrest consequences to that individual to break the smuggling cycle and end the subject's desire to attempt further illegal entry. The CDS is a means of standardizing the decision-making process regarding the application of consequences and provides for the evaluation of outcome effectiveness. Consequences delivered under this system that execute targeted enforcement techniques range from administrative, criminal prosecution, and programmatic elements that are designed to impact and change the way TCOs conduct business and stem the flow of illegal activity.

Objective 1.4

Whole-of-Government Approach

The U.S. Border Patrol will continue to integrate targeting practices and joint operations with CBP's Office of Field Operations (OFO) and Office of Air and Marine (OAM) to better achieve its goals. The Border Patrol also will work with its Federal, state, local, and tribal law enforcement partners to achieve a holistic approach to border security. This is accomplished by establishing a unity of purpose; advancing operational integration and jointly planned targeted operations; developing intelligence and accomplishing intelligence fusion;

and creating integrated partnerships. This whole-of-government approach, coupled with the application of the principles of targeted enforcement, consequence delivery, and operational discipline, provides the capability necessary to enhance the abilities of the Border Patrol and its partners to address threats or emergencies within a region.

Operation Stonegarden

Operation Stonegarden is a DHS-funded, CBP-facilitated operation designed to enhance border security by developing a multilateral enforcement effort between the Border Patrol and state, local, and tribal law enforcement agencies (SLT). Border Patrol sectors coordinate operations based on enhanced border security through an increased SLT presence along the Southwest, Northern, and Coastal Borders.

State, County, and Local Task Forces

Members of the Border Patrol are assigned to various counter-narcotics and counter-crime/terrorism task forces at the local law enforcement level. These task forces work on drug and violent crimes associated with

trafficking that affect the border communities and concentrate on providing a coordinated response to disrupt, degrade, and defeat terrorist and criminal organizations.

Federal Task Forces

Recognizing the jurisdictional complexity of the border environment, partnerships with the Border Patrol's Federal counterparts are essential for the Border Patrol to achieve its goals. These partnerships are critical at the operational and tactical levels, as well as at the

strategic and policy levels, where the Border Patrol must coordinate policies and ensure adherence to relevant laws and regulations. The Border Patrol has further strengthened its law enforcement partnerships along the border by colocating and integrating its assets and personnel with other law enforcement organizations and offering reciprocal opportunities consistent with applicable laws and authorities. The nature of shared communities and shared infrastructure requires that the Border Patrol's approach further develops and enhances a unity of effort between CBP and all its Federal partners.

Border Patrol Special Coordination Center

The Border Patrol Special Coordination Center (BPSCC) is a critical program in the Border Patrol's adoption of a whole-of-government approach to law enforcement. The BPSCC acts as a liaison between the Border Patrol and the Department of Defense (DOD) through Joint Task Force-North (JTF-North). The center is colocated with JTF-North at Fort Bliss, El Paso, Texas, and serves as the focus of efforts to synchronize DOD support to law enforcement and the Border Patrol's strategic goals and objectives.

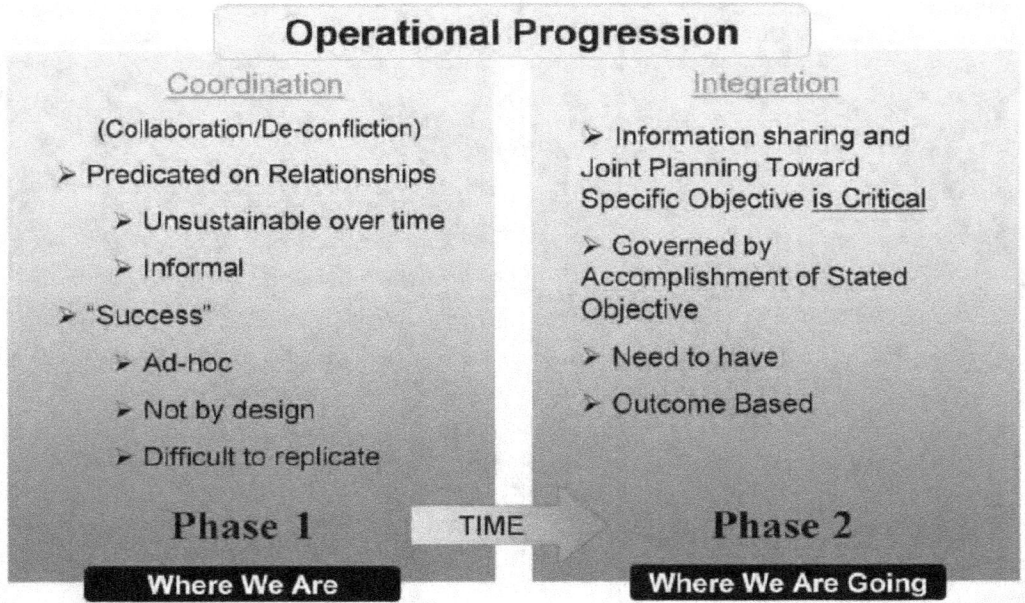

Comprehensive Approach

CBP builds coalitions with international, Federal, state, local, and tribal law enforcement agencies, public-service entities, and other identified stakeholders to develop a common operational strategy in the border environment. This approach requires continued integration within CBP of Border Patrol, OFO, and OAM operations. This approach ensures unity of effort and maximum enforcement benefits from combined resources and allows for the secure flow of goods and people moving toward and intending to enter the United States. The Border Patrol mission involves a multitude of entities working together in a seamless and integrated way to prevent terrorism and transnational threats at the earliest opportunity. That cooperation ensures our Nations' shared communities, critical infrastructure, and populations are mutually prepared and protected through bi-national and bilateral security, resilience, and response protocols.

Objective 1.5

Increase Community Engagement

The Border Patrol will continue to use its collective capabilities to engage and educate the public about border activities and issues so the Border Patrol can leverage the critical assistance of border communities.

Reduce Crime and Violence

Engagement by the Border Patrol with local law enforcement and the public can lower crime and reduce violence.

Operation Detour

Operation Detour is a community outreach program conducted in conjunction with local school systems, which began in the Border Patrol's Del Rio Sector in Texas and has expanded along the Southwest Border. Operation Detour is a public-service campaign targeted at middle- and high-school students in an effort to educate them and our community about the dangers and consequences surrounding narcotics smuggling. Students are encouraged to think for themselves, withstand peer pressure, and reach out to parents, teachers, counselors, or law enforcement if they are asked to work for a TCO.

Drug Demand Reduction

Drug Demand Reduction Programs are public-service campaigns targeted at the community's youth (ages 14-18) in an effort to educate them and the community about the dangers and consequences of drug use and involvement with drug trafficking and criminal organizations. Focusing on the youth of the community, these programs use graphic depictions, video, and live discussion to provide a true sense of the horrors and tragedies that befall individuals and families that become involved with narcotics smuggling and the narco-terrorism underworld.

Community and Stakeholder Outreach

External messaging through proactive media releases, interviews, and ride-alongs are provided to local, national and international press, and other community stakeholders to show the operational reality in communities along the border. Stakeholders are educated through briefings, tours, informal meetings, and stakeholder academies. Some existing programs include the Border Patrol Heroes Project, the Border Patrol History Project, the Border Community Liaison Program, Ranch Liaison, Citizens Academies, town-hall meetings, and the Explorers. The dissemination of operational achievements and challenges is essential to foster support from our partners and stakeholders.

Congressional Staffer Academy

The purpose of the Congressional Staffer Academy is to educate and inform staff from key Congressional offices or committees with an interest in and oversight of CBP regarding the Strategic Plan, capabilities, challenges, achievements, and the future of its three main operational components, including the Border Patrol. The Border Patrol's continued participation in the Congressional Staffer Academy provides Congressional staff members with a unique opportunity to travel to the front lines and receive a first-hand overview of the practical instruction and skills taught to agents, while featuring specific field locations that highlight CBP's layered approach to national security.

Border Community Liaison

The purpose of the Border Community Liaison Program is to facilitate the national expansion of relationships and interactions among government, law enforcement, non-government agencies, border-community partners, and the Border Patrol. The program provides stakeholders with a designated point of contact at their respective Border Patrol sector and encourages communication between the Border Patrol and its border-community partners.

Citizens Academy

The Citizens Academy informs the public about the organizational structure of DHS, CBP, and the Border Patrol. It is designed to provide the community with an overview of the complex and challenging enforcement skills taught to all new Border Patrol agents at the Border Patrol Academy, in addition to insight into the daily challenges Border Patrol agents face as they perform their duties. Participants have the opportunity to experience hands-on training in firearms and Border Patrol operations. The classes provide an in-depth understanding of the history of the Border Patrol, its strategic plans and mission, immigration, canine and checkpoint authority, and demonstrations of felony stops, as well as search and seizure.

Goal 2: Strengthen the Border Patrol

The U.S. Border Patrol must continue to mature, refine, and integrate its capabilities and techniques. To meet current and future operational and organizational requirements, it is essential to develop, deploy, and manage institutional capabilities within the Border Patrol. This includes areas such as human-capital management, training, leadership development, employee support, organizational integrity, doctrine development, and technology research and development.

Objective 2.1

Strengthen Investment in People

People are our most valuable asset. The Border Patrol must hire the most qualified applicants and train new employees to be successful in performing the mission. Leaders must ensure that employees have the opportunity to reach their highest potential by receiving the appropriate education, training, and work experiences to progress in the organization.

Invest in People

The U.S. Border Patrol is advancing its human-capital management strategy to ensure that there is a systematic and deliberative process to select the right employee, at the right time, for the right position. The Border Patrol will use a multi-tiered approach incorporating education, training and work experience to maximize the effectiveness of Border Patrol personnel. Components of the strategy include:

Succession Management

Succession management will incorporate the necessary education, training, and work experiences to continually develop and hone Border Patrol employees' knowledge, skills, and abilities. Career maps will communicate the necessary experiences employees must obtain to remain competitive for future advancement.

Targeted Placement

The Border Patrol will use targeted placement to offer employees progressive leadership and program-management experiences to prepare them for positions of greater responsibility. To select the best qualified employees, the Border Patrol will identify the necessary knowledge, skills, and abilities for key leadership positions and match the employee's qualifications. For future placement, employees will not only be evaluated on their current performance, they will be evaluated on their future potential.

Advanced Education and Training

The Border Patrol will grow the pool of applicants for advanced education and training through an agency-wide campaign to increase awareness of available programs. When employees complete the advanced programs, targeted placement will leverage their skills and abilities.

Joint and Inter-Agency Assignments

Temporary joint- and inter-agency assignments enhance an employee's professional development and agency capabilities. Employees learn critical management and planning skills through diverse assignments. The Border Patrol will benefit from the cross-pollination of best practices, increased awareness of agency goals, and the holistic understanding of border security and homeland security.

Mentoring

Reorganization and expansion of the Border Patrol's mentoring program will enable institutional knowledge to be passed from mature, experienced agents to newly promoted and future potential leaders.

Objective 2.2

Support Border Patrol Employees

The U.S. Border Patrol has a long history of supporting its employees and has been a leader within CBP in the development of robust employee-support programs. Continuing on that tradition and recognizing the inherent dangers of law enforcement work, the Border Patrol continues to look for new ways to support employees.

Deliver Responsive Employee-Support Programs

The nature of law enforcement guarantees exposure to stressful and traumatic incidents. It is incumbent upon leadership to provide ways for Border Patrol employees to remain resilient in the performance of their day-to-day duties.

National Critical Incident Response Team

As mobility continues to be an integral part of the Border Patrol's day-to-day operations, attention must be given to minimize the impact on employees' well-being. The National Critical Incident Response Team (NCIRT), a component of the Border Patrol's Traumatic Incident Management Plan, supports CBP employees involved in small- and large-scale, critical-incident operations. The team consists of Peer Support members, Chaplains, and mental-health professionals who have specialized training in critical-incident-response management. Victims of traumatic events, as well as those responding to them, may be prone to certain reactions. When left unaddressed, they can result in negative, long-term consequences. NCIRT provides affected employees with a targeted stress-management program to assist in recovery from exposure to traumatic events.

Employee Comportment and Resilience Committee

Employee comportment (i.e., personal integrity and conduct) and resilience (i.e., ability to recover readily from adversity) are key factors in the Border Patrol's ability to effectively execute the mission. The Border Patrol will evaluate and determine the qualitative variables that enable mission success, sustain high morale, and promote a professional, healthy, and robust workforce. Leaders will leverage all necessary resources to develop and maintain a resilient culture, as well as promote personal integrity and adherence to CBP's standards of conduct.

Objective 2.3

Preserve Organizational Integrity

The U.S. Border Patrol is fortunate in that the documented cases of corrupt employees represent only a minute percentage of the workforce. However, any instance of corruption within our ranks always has been – and always will be – unacceptable.

Anti-Corruption

The Border Patrol will continue to actively reduce the potential for corruption. Leaders must set the example and promote integrity throughout the Border Patrol. Leaders will immediately address issues, or the perception of an issue, as they arise. Components of the strategy include participation in internal and CBP-level integrity review committees.

Integrity Advisory Committee

The Integrity Advisory Committee (IAC) provides strategic recommendations to combat corruption and promote integrity among all Border Patrol employees. The committee includes a select group of Border Patrol field and Headquarters personnel, as well as advisors and subject-matter experts from CBP component offices of Internal Affairs, Chief Counsel, and Human Resources Management, as well as the Office of Field Operations (OFO).

Participation in the Commissioner's Integrity Planning and Coordination Cell

The Border Patrol participates in the Commissioner's Integrity Planning and Coordination Cell (IPCC), which reviews integrity-related efforts throughout CBP. In addition, the Border Patrol works with OFO's Analytical Management Systems Control Office to assess the feasibility of using agent-related anomalies in various CBP systems as indicators of potential integrity issues.

Objective 2.4
Improve Organizational Structures, Processes, Systems, and Doctrine

As the Border Patrol grows and matures, it is necessary to codify best practices and policies to ensure that the organization continues to provide professional border-enforcement capability for the United States.

Enhancing the Organization

As the Border Patrol continues to mature and grow into the 21st century, the selection and application of doctrinal planning processes are required. There are numerous techniques available for tactical, operational, and strategic planning. Border Patrol agents must recognize the differences in these types of planning and adopt the appropriate ones for the situation. While an agent educated in these planning processes should serve in a planning capacity, his or her career path should not be restricted to such assignments – rather these assignments should be seen as a stepping stone to achieving higher-level field commands.

Developing and institutionalizing doctrine within the organization will help execute the long-term strategy and enable the Border Patrol to operate on a standard that captures necessary change and allows operations to function smoothly. Border Patrol Headquarters will develop doctrine as a process to seamlessly link the operating force to emerging tactics, techniques, and procedures, as well as best practices, while additionally focusing on enduring principles and techniques. Doctrine will focus on overarching enduring principles, sector operations, and future border-security initiatives that all agents can use to execute their mission in the field.

Reorganize and Realign Headquarters for Maximum Efficiency

The Border Patrol is modifying its Table of Organization, which will delineate the chain of command and identify each Border Patrol agent and operational support position. The Table of Organization enhances the Border Patrol's ability to make critical resource allocation and prioritization decisions, thereby aligning staff resources to achieve maximum mission effectiveness.

Standardize Organizational Structures for Sector Headquarters and Stations

The Border Patrol standardized the organizational structures for the Northern, Coastal and Southwest border sector headquarters and stations. The organizational structure creates uniformity in how sectors and stations are organized throughout the Border Patrol, aligns functions throughout sector headquarters, establishes a unified command for station management at the sector headquarters, supports succession management with progressive leadership opportunities, and creates a path to station and executive leadership positions.

Objective 2.5

Enhance Overall Efficiency of the Border Patrol

It is the Border Patrol's responsibility to ensure that its leaders, agents, and support personnel are good stewards of American tax dollars.

Executive Governance Board

The Border Patrol requires a governance structure to ensure that its investments are in alignment with the vision, strategic goals, and overall mission priorities of the agency. Border Patrol Headquarters has established an executive governance forum to provide awareness of, advocacy for, and collaboration on current and future investments. The Executive Governance Board will be implemented using standardized implementation methodologies to achieve substantive improvement in key interdivisional and sector business processes. The organization must ensure that its investments in capabilities, including existing systems, equipment, and resources align with the vision, strategic goals, and overall mission priorities of the agency. The board is composed of leadership from each division within U.S. Border Patrol Headquarters.

Establishing Measures of Performance

As the Border Patrol progresses toward organizational rigor and maturity, an essential element will be the development and continual refinement of comprehensive, demanding, and results-driven performance measures that hold us to account. Even as the organization internalizes these standards, it also must effectively communicate overall performance to its most important stakeholders – the American public. Initiatives such as the Border Condition Index (BCI) may facilitate this communication. Accountability for each of the objectives

in the Strategic Plan means the Border Patrol is developing – and in many cases will report publicly – measures of performance and indicators of impact in areas including:

- The ability to direct appropriate levels of capability to identified high-risk areas along the Nation's borders;
- Improved situational awareness and detection capabilities;
- Effective response times, mobility, and manpower efficiencies;
- Apprehension of those who seek to enter the country illegally, as well as seizures of contraband;
- Contributions to disrupting the smuggling cycle through systematic delivery of consequences to those apprehended;
- Delivery of tangible impacts that help reduce border-related crime and violence;
- Outreach and cooperation with the public;
- The ability to engage a strong workforce through hiring, learning opportunities, and key support programs;
- Development and integration of self-evaluation processes to ensure adherence to missions, goals, and objectives;
- Implementation of environmentally sound and resource-efficient plans of action; and
- Institutionalization of cost-saving practices.

The Border Condition Index is an index currently under development that captures a comprehensive picture of border conditions. The BCI includes important indicators of activity between the ports of entry; indicators of the amount, nature and flow of traffic at the ports of entry; and quality of life indicators in border communities.

Ultimately, the Border Patrol will secure the Nation's land borders between the ports of entry against all threats as part of the larger CBP, DHS, and whole-of-government effort. Leveraging all available actions, programs, and techniques encompassed within this Strategic Plan, the Border Patrol will prevent terrorists from entering the United States and disrupt and prevent Transnational Criminal Organizations from conducting smuggling and criminal activities along the border. This Strategic Plan will strengthen the Border Patrol to achieve increased capability and promote innovative interagency cooperation to border security operations, as well as secure the border through the use of **Information, Integration and Rapid Response.**

Connectivity Between DHS, CBP, and U.S. Border Patrol National Strategies

CBP FY 2009-14 Strategic Plan / Missions, Goals, and Priorities, FY 2011-2013

VISION
Securing the Nation's Borders while facilitating legitimate trade and travel

Goal 1: Secure the Nation's Border

OBJ 1.2 Risk-Based Approach to detect and prevent the entry of hazardous materials, goods, and instruments of terror into the United States.

OBJ 1.3 Risk-Based Approach to detect and prevent the entry of dangerous people into the United States

OBJ 1.4 Provide training and resources to address a wide range of critical missions

MG&P Goal 3.1: Enhance Integrity Programs and Identify, Develop, and Train New Leaders

OBJ 1.4 Provide training and resources to address a wide range of critical missions

MG&P Goal 3.2: Integrate CBP as an Organization to Enhance Effectiveness

2012-2016 U.S. Border Patrol Strategic Plan

VISION
Risk-Based Approach to Border Security using Information, Integration and Rapid Response Capabilities

Goal 1: Secure America's Borders

OBJ 1.1 Prevent Terrorists and Terrorist Weapons from Entering the United States

OBJ 1.2 Manage Risk

OBJ 1.3 Disrupt and Degrade Transnational Criminal Organizations

OBJ 1.4 Whole-of-Government Approach

OBJ 1.5 Increase Community Engagement

Goal 2: Strengthen the Border Patrol

OBJ 2.1 Strengthen Investment in People

OBJ 2.2 Support Border Patrol Employees

OBJ 2.3 Preserve Organizational Integrity

OBJ 2.4 Improve Organizational Structures, Processes, Systems and Doctrine

OBJ 2.5 Enhance Overall Efficiency of the Border Patrol

Quadrennial Homeland Security Review (FEB 2010)

VISION
A homeland that is safe, secure, and resilient against terrorism and other hazards where American interests, aspirations and way of life can thrive.

Goal 2.1 Effectively Control U.S. Air, Land and Sea

Goal 1.1 Prevent Terrorist Attacks

Goal 1.3 Manage Risks to Critical Infrastructure, Key Leadership and Events

Goal 2.3 Disrupt and Dismantle Transnational Criminal Organizations

Goal 2.1 Effectively Control U.S. Air, Land and Sea

Glossary

Comprehensive Approach – Integrates the cooperative efforts of the departments and agencies of the U.S. Government, intergovernmental and nongovernmental organizations, multinational partners, and private sector entities to achieve unity of effort toward a common goal.

Degrade – To reduce in worth or value; to fall below a normal state; deteriorate; to significantly impair structure or function.

Disrupt – To throw into confusion or disorder, or to interrupt or impede the progress, movement, or procedure of a person or organization involved in criminal activity.

Information – Raw, unanalyzed data that may identify threats, vulnerabilities or risks. Information collected is considered "raw data" until its sources have been evaluated, corroborated or analyzed through due diligence methodologies to obtain added value for planning purposes.

Integrated Mission Analysis – Operational and intelligence tools that allow Border Patrol Headquarters to identify and prioritize critical threats and vulnerabilities to determine unacceptable risks to border security requiring action or response to mitigate them.

Integration – The act of combining lessons learned, best practices, capabilities, and emerging policy/strategy to be more agile and flexible toward changes within the context of executing the U.S. Border Patrol mission in conjunction with partners.

Integrity Advisory Committee – The Integrity Advisory Committee, which includes a select group of Border Patrol field and Headquarters personnel, as well as advisors and subject-matter experts from CBP components, provides strategic recommendations to combat corruption and promote integrity among all Border Patrol employees.

Rapid Response – Immediate planning and/or action taken to mitigate emerging threats.

Risk – Assessed probability for an unwanted outcome based on an assessment of the threat originator. This is measured against the capabilities of the threat originator to carry out that threat and the severity of the potential consequences.

Targeted Enforcement – Leveraging all available assets against a specific action, area, individual, or organization and using those deemed most appropriate to mitigate risk.

Transnational Criminal Organization (TCO) – Group activities of three or more persons, with hierarchical links or personal relationships that permit group leaders to earn profits (or control territories or markets – internal or foreign) by means of violence, intimidation, or corruption to advance criminal activity or infiltrate the legitimate economy.

Threat – Information expressing intent to conduct illegal activity (often derived from intelligence) coupled with the capability of a specific event or series of events, or observation of suspicious activity.

Vulnerability – The protective measures in place are less than the protective measures needed to mitigate risk.

Whole-of-Government – The idea that U.S. Government national security partners should develop plans and conduct operations from a shared perspective and shared resources to enable mission accomplishment.